Ma Frump's
Cultural Guide to Plastic Gardening

Books by Marcia Muth

A World Set Apart—Memory Paintings

Is It Safe To Drink The Water? A Guide To Santa Fe

How To Paint & Sell Your Art

Kachinas: A Selected Bibliography

Writing And Selling Poetry, Fiction, Articles, Plays and Local History

Thin Ice And Other Poems

Indian Pottery Of The Southwest: A Selected Bibliography

Sticks And Stones And Other Poems

Words And Images

Ma Frump's
Cultural Guide to Plastic Gardening

A Humorous Guide to Colorful
All-Season Gardening
with Plastic Plants
and Flowers

New and Improved Edition

Text & Illustrations
by
Marcia Muth

SANTA FE

© 2008 by Marcia Muth. All rights reserved.

No part of this book may be reproduced in any form or by any electronic or mechanical means including information storage and retrieval systems without permission in writing from the publisher, except by a reviewer who may quote brief passages in a review.

Sunstone books may be purchased for educational, business, or sales promotional use. For information please write: Special Markets Department, Sunstone Press, P.O. Box 2321, Santa Fe, New Mexico 87504-2321.

Book and Cover design by Vicki Ahl
Body typeface is Verdana 12/18 ✸ Display typeface is Eras ITC

Library of Congress Cataloging-in-Publication Data

Muth, Marcia, 1919-
  Ma Frump's cultural guide to plastic gardening : a humorous guide to colorful, all-season gardening with plastic plants and flowers / text & illustrations by Marcia Muth. -- New and improved ed.
       p. cm.
  ISBN 978-0-86534-611-6 (softcover : alk. paper)
 1. Gardening. 2. Artificial flowers. I. Title. II. Title: Cultural guide to plastic gardening. III. Title: Humorous guide to colorful, all-season gardening with plastic plants and flowers.
  SB454.M88 2008
  635.902'07--dc22
                                                    2008009128

WWW.SUNSTONEPRESS.COM
SUNSTONE PRESS / POST OFFICE BOX 2321 / SANTA FE, NM 87504-2321 /USA
(505) 988-4418 / ORDERS ONLY (800) 243-5644 / FAX (505) 988-1025

**Dedicated to Kay Lockridge
and
Roslyn Kitty Pulitzer**

Who are traditional gardeners but understand the plastic gardener.

Ma Frump happily at work in her opulent garden.

Contents

Foreword ____ ____ ____ ____ ____ 9
Why Plastic Gardening? ____ ____ ____ 11
Your Garden Wardrobe ____ ____ ____ 15
Garden Tools And Other Equipment ____ 17
When And What To Plant ____ ____ ____ 22
How To Plant ____ ____ ____ ____ ____ 26
Gardening In Special Geographical Regions 30
Garden Loveliness ____ ____ ____ ____ 32
The Garden Pool ____ ____ ____ ____ 35
Vegetable And Fruit Plastic Gardening ____ 38
Wintertime Gardening ____ ____ ____ 43
The 21st Century Plastic Gardener _ ____ 46
How To Store ____ ____ ____ ____ ____ 48
Garden Accessories_ ____ ____ ____ 53
The Complete Plastic Gardener and Her
   (Or His) Garden _ ____ ____ ____ ____ 55

Foreword

When I wrote the book over thirty years ago, it was intended simply as a light-hearted, fun look at gardening. The new edition is still that but now there is a serious undertone. I did not realize the true importance of plastic gardening until a newspaper columnist, Denise Kusel, wrote in *The Santa Fe New Mexican* that I was helping conserve water by promoting plastic gardening not just as a novelty but a necessity.

What makes this edition new and improved? Times have changed and there are new techniques, new products and new suggestions for your very own personal approach to "garden loveliness." Finally, if "new and improved" works for cereal, headache pills and lounge chairs—why not for Ma Frump also?

Although I have continued to use the term "plastic" in the book, gardeners now have access to metal flowers and other garden helps which will be discussed in the following pages. It is the spirit of artificiality that counts!

—Ma Frump
(occasionally known as "Marcia Muth")

Why Plastic Gardening?

I have often been asked, "Why plastic gardening?" This is a question frequently asked my by friends, acquaintances and even strangers! I have become accustomed not only to the question, but to the exclamations and expressions of wonderment when my garden is viewed. Just the other day a friend asked, "How can you do it?"

It would be easy to remain modest about my gardening methods, but friends have prevailed upon me to share my gardening concepts with the world at large. I can only hope that you, my readers, will get as much pleasure and happiness from your plastic garden as I get from mine. This is why I have used the word "cultural" in connection with this kind of gardening, for it is a cultural experience as well as a way of beautifying the world around you.

Plastic gardening is the gardening of the

future right now! It has many advantages and the most important is that it is ecologically sound! No need to wonder any more how you can do your bit for the troubled earth! No, now you can plant your plastic garden and hold your head up in any ecology group. Just think of it—plastic gardens do not have to be watered. They do not take valuable nutriments from the soil. They never require any applications of sprays or dangerous insecticide powders. Plastic gardens are the answer to the ecologist's nightmare and the gardener's dream of eternal perfection.

There are other advantages to plastic gardening. Plastic flowers and plants do not rot. Their leaves never wilt and drop off just before your big garden party. Plastic plants are not attacked by the blight or by suspicious looking bugs. Other pests are also put off by plastic plants. Rabbits have been observed in a test garden to absolutely ignore plastic plants and go immediately to a natural plant and eat it down to the ground. Large dogs and cats also ignore plastic plants as being of little interest to them, but puppies, I regret to say, have a tendency to play with both plastic and natural flowers and plants. However, you can, as I have done, teach your puppy the difference between your plastic flowers and your neighbor's natural garden. In time, and with patience on your part, your puppy can learn to be as discriminating as you are about plants.

There is also sound medical practice in having a plastic garden. Because there is no irritating pollen, there is also no problem with allergies. One friend who could never go out without carrying a large box of Kleenex because of her various allergies to plants now spends many happy hours in her plastic garden.

Granted there is an initial outlay, but there is where it stops! You do not have to buy bags of fertilizer which are both expensive and prone to burst in the back of the trunk, making a mess. You do not have to buy sprays, plant foods or dangerous poisons. The latter has other disadvantages, for how will you explain the bottle or jar of poison if a murder takes place in the vicinity? You may claim you bought it for the mildew on your geraniums or the 'black spot' on your roses, but can you prove it? Don't risk the embarrassment of a trip to the local police station. Stick with plastic gardening and you will never have any of those horrid bottles with skull and crossbone labels in your gardening shed or garage.

You will not need to purchase a lot of expensive and various tools, either. As you will see in my section on Garden Tools and Other Equipment, only a minimum of tools is needed for successful plastic gardening. The money you will save on a lawn mower (if you plant plastic grass) will pay for a vacation so you can visit other gardens and look with enjoyment, knowing that you have none of the work to do.

Yes, plastic gardening is the answer to your gardening problems, and it has this final advantage: It takes up much less of your time. There is no pruning, no trimming, no watering, no cutting—only enjoyment. You can spend as much or as little time as you wish. I know some devotees of plastic gardening who put in their gardens at the beginning of the season (the spring) and never look at them again. But, there are others, and I am one of them, who spend a little time each day relaxing among the plastic flowers and shrubs.

Plastic gardening is for the modern individual!

Your Garden Wardrobe

Fortunately with plastic gardening, you need only a small wardrobe. Since plastic gardening requires only minimal time to keep it up, you will not have to spend hours outdoors in the hot sun.

You will need a hat. This should be a hat with a wide brim to protect you from the sun.

You can decorate the hat with ribbons, buttons or flowers. Express your personality through your choice of hat and decorations. You will want gloves. While you will not be dealing with thorns, you might come across a funny bug or worm. Also, you will be planting your flowers in real dirt. Garden gloves now come in attractive colors and designs. There is no longer the need to wear gray or brown gloves and look dowdy. Don't wear open-toe sandals. You do want to look like a serious gardener, and besides you will be using scissors and other garden tools and you could get hurt. I always wear sturdy shoes in the garden thus making a good impression on passers-by plus I don't want strange insects crawling across my toes. Shorts? Shorts really depend on your body type. Remember even plastic gardening requires a lot of kneeling and bending.

    By the way, there's no need to be isolated from the world when gardening. Recently I saw in a catalog a belt pack in which you can put your phone and a small garden tool. It also had room for a notepad and pencil. This way you can write down any messages you get or thoughts you might have while gardening.

Garden Tools and Other Equipment

As I pointed out at the beginning of this book, plastic gardening does not require a lot of tools and equipment. You can do your gardening with just a few basic tools. Naturally, if you wish to have an elaborate array of gardening tools you may, but why not spend the money on other necessities such as books, banana splits, movies, and trips to the Caribbean? And, of course, the number of tools required will depend upon how involved your plastic gardening becomes. A good rule to remember is, "extensive equals expensive."

From my years of experience at practical plastic gardening, here is a list of tools:

>*Green Paint*—Since nature has seen fit to make green the predominating color, you will need a can of green paint to touch

up your plastic leaves, trees, and grass when fading occurs.

Knee Pads—Kneeling directly on the ground can be very tiring and painful. These pads will cushion your bones. Not only that, they will make you look like a serious dirt gardener. Knee pads are also great for hiding knobby knees.

Paint Kit—In addition to the green paint already mentioned, you will want a small kit of assorted colors to keep your plastic flower blooms in bright shades. A word of caution—be sure to select waterproof paint or you may be in for an unpleasant surprise after the first rain.

Pliers—You will find pliers to be one of your most useful tools. Small pliers will do, but advanced plastic flower gardeners often have two pliers of varying sizes. You will use pliers to cut the wire stems of plants and flowers. They are also useful for bending and shaping the thicker and heavier plants.

Pots and Flower Boxes—Have a number of different sizes and colors. Buy only those of plastic manufacture.

Rake—Useful for removing debris from plastic grass or arranging gravel.

Scissors—Like pliers, scissors are an indispensable piece of plastic gardening equipment. Choose a medium size pair which is sturdy. Be sure to keep the cutting edge sharp. It is very difficult to cut plastic with a dull pair of scissors. Scissors are used for trimming ragged edges, cutting thin stems and snipping labels.

Scotch Tape—Tape is used for minor repairs to stems, leaves and petals.

Shovel—Used to plant large plastic shrubs and trees.

Stapler and Staples—Staples are used to make repairs to plants and flowers in cases where tape would not prove strong enough. A suggestion—check your stapler before going out to garden. It is very irritating to be out of staples just as you have your broken leaf properly positioned.

Storage Boxes—You will need storage boxes in proportion to the number of plastic plants, flowers, fruits and vegetables used in your garden. During winter months and rotation periods, your unused plants, flowers, fruits and vegetables are kept in these storage boxes (See my section on How To Store).

Trowel—A rather conventional garden tool, but needed to dig small holes if your soil is not such that you can jam your plastic flowers directly into the ground without artificial aids.

Watering Can—While you will not need to water your flowers, you may sometimes need to moisturize the planting area. It can be surprising how hard and unyielding dirt can become. A watering can prominently displayed provides the right touch of authenticity to your garden.

Wire—Choose a pliable wire unless you are very strong. Wire is useful for bracing limp plants, tying plastic fruit or blossoms to trees and bushes and for fastening your plastic vegetables to vines.

This, then, is your basic list, but you may want to use other tools. For example, I know one lady who does all of her plastic gardening with just three instruments, a pair of scissors, a plastic spoon, and a spatula.

When and What to Plant

It is very important to know when to plant your plastic flowers. You do not, after all, wish to appear to be lacking in common sense by putting out flowers that are inappropriate to the season. Of course, *what* you plant and *when* you plant will be determined by your geographical region. There are particular times for particular flowers and you should be aware of what should be done, and when.

One way is to read the weekly garden column in your local paper and see what is to be done that week. When it mentions that certain flowers are in bloom, be sure that your garden is well supplied with those flowers.

Another way of discovery is to peek over the fence at your neighbor's natural garden and see what is in bloom. For example, you can quickly plant *your* daffodils when you see those first signs of yellow in her yard. There is really no particular virtue in being the first in your neighborhood to break out with daffodils, crocuses or other spring flowers. Take your time and be sure that you are planting the right plastic flowers at the right time.

This brings me to another point about plastic flowers—their immunity from frost. For many years I have seen my neighbors' gardens come to early bloom only to be blackened and withered by a sudden cold frost while my own plastic flowers are nodding happily and colorfully in the crisp March air.

A method I recommend is the keeping of a plastic planting diary or notebook. After you have once gone through the complete cycle of a year, you will have all the information you need about what and when to plant at your fingertips. You can avoid costly and embarrassing mistakes—unlike the unfortunate plastic flower gardener who planted her blooming tulips in September instead of April. She reported that the crowd of curious nature lovers that was attracted by this spectacle was more of a nuisance than a pleasure.

It is also wise to be cautious about planting plastic plants and flowers which are not native to your area. You may be subject to some ridicule if you have orchids in your garden and these are not plants which are indigenous to your locale. As a friend remarked to me recently, "There is a fine line between the exotic and the bizarre." If you prefer exotic plants and flowers, keep them in your indoor plastic flower greenhouse or use them for house plants.

Rotate your plants as the season progresses. When the time comes for natural droop and decay, whisk your flowers out of the ground or pot and put them into storage. Remember, a great part of the success in plastic gardening lies in staying close to the natural order of things even while you are *improving* upon that natural order.

A garden plot plan will cut down on the time you spend wondering what to plant where. Make a diagram of your garden area and select your flowers and plants before you put them out. You can see at a glance how colors will mix and blend. It will also help you to avoid the mistake made by many natural gardeners who are upset to find that they have somehow planted all the tall flowers in the front of their beds and the smaller ones in the back. You must agree that it is very irritating to find irises in the front, hiding your nasturtiums and pansies! This is, of course, never a problem to the plastic flower gardener.

If you should make an error in your garden plot plan, you can still remedy it after planting time is over by simply rearranging your plants or flowers in better or more suitable places. Unlike your neighbor, you will not have to worry about roots or plant shock.

After experimentation you may find that you have developed the perfect garden and that you wish to keep the arrangements you have made but without leaving your flowers out when the season is past. You can solve this problem by taking pictures of your gardens and drawing careful diagrams. Oh yes, be sure to use color film. The next year and the year afterward, and for as many years as you like, you can have the same lovely garden.

Remember, your plastic garden should be a fun place without the anxieties that go with natural gardens and without all that back-breaking work.

How To Plant

When you have made your decision about what you want to plant and where you are going to plant, you are ready for the big step of actually doing it. I can tell you that it is a thrilling day when you step outside with your plastic flowers, your garden tools and your garden plot plan! I find it helpful to carry my garden tools in a little plastic bucket.

At your planting site, select the flowers or plants which are to be put in that area. With your scissors remove the paper labels attached to each flower. If the label gives the name of the flower, you may wish to leave that part intact, but be sure that you have cut off the price, place of manufacturing and name of manufacturer. The sight of flowers with little tags that say, "Made in China—89¢" does not add to your garden beauty. I say this in warning because I

have seen instances where stares of admiration turned to snickers of derision when tags were not removed.

Tags removed—your flowers are ready to be planted. With pliers or scissors, cut the stems so that you have flowers of varying lengths. Remember: it is important to avoid monotony in your garden; therefore, you won't want all your flowers to be the same length. Cut some short and some long.

Choose your colors carefully and you will have a garden that is pleasing to the eye. Your neighbors with natural gardens will be chagrined when they see how well *your* colors come out while *they* are at the mercy of seeds and bulbs that do not always match the colors depicted on the package. In plastic gardening, you know what you are planting!

Another nice feature about plastic gardening is that there is none of this tiresome waiting for things to grow and bloom. You can go out and plant your garden at two o'clock and sit down to tea at three, feasting your eyes on a rainbow of colors.

Group your flowers in attractive beds. I prefer to use both ground planting and pot or planter arrangements for my plastic gardening. It makes for a nice variety. For example, I have a rose bed with several attractive varieties of plastic roses, three plastic planters with multi-colored plastic creeping phlox, bleeding hearts and snapdragons. Around the patio in pots and round planters I have geraniums, delphiniums and petunias. In my back yard I have giant plastic sunflowers, clumps of plastic violets and sweet peas. I also recommend plastic periwinkle, red sedum and pansies for added spots of garden color. Of course, the list is endless, and you can select the flowers that give you the most visual satisfaction.

Gardening In Special Geographical Regions

Although most people live in areas of the country where gardening is easy, there are thousands who live in other places where the weather, altitude or some other natural nonsense interferes with normal gardening habits. While we may dream of the days of the future when we can live in the all-controlled plastic environment, we have to live in the present right now. Therefore, I will discuss briefly some of the problems involving gardening in special geographical regions.

High altitude gardening poses far less of a problem for the plastic flower gardener than it does for the natural gardener. You will, of course, have a shorter growing season, which means you may want to put your gardening emphasis on indoor plants. A plastic flower greenhouse will give you many hours of pleasure. Usually,

I recommend to high altitude gardeners that they go in for plastic shrubs and imitation rock formations.

Desert gardening is very hot and dry. You won't want to spend a lot of time out in the sun. Concentrate your gardening efforts on a nice, plastic cactus bed. Place the bed where you can easily see it from inside your air-conditioned living room. A few plastic lizards and some plastic bones will add touches of enchanting realism to your garden scene.

Sea level gardening is just the opposite of high altitude gardening. You will enjoy having lush, tropical plastic flowers in your sea level garden unless, of course, you don't live in the tropics. If you live at sea level but in the north, you will have to make the necessary gardening adjustments.

North or south, I do recommend the use of sea shells as an added decorative feature in your sea level garden. While it is more desirable to use plastic sea shells, you may substitute real ones if you are unable to purchase the other kind. I am sure, though, that if you try, you can find some strands of plastic seaweed to drape around your garden.

Garden Loveliness

Garden loveliness is the term I use to describe the garden which has more than plastic flowers in it. I am talking now about those lovely gardens which are filled with plastic statuary, fences and other charming accessories.

When the first edition of this book was published, there was very little available in the way of suitable garden accessories. But times have changed! Almost every gardening catalog I see has some items that can add color and interest to your garden. There are artificial life-like birds that range from the ever popular flamingoes to our favorite songbirds. There are reproductions of domestic and semi-wild animals. Gnomes are still a popular item. No longer are they just standing or sitting but you can get them in a variety of poses and with special added features, such as carrying little

solar lanterns that light up at night. Just think how magical that will make your garden look!

Your choice of statuary should reflect both your personality and your environment. You may want to have some ducks, geese or even donkeys in your garden. I have known other gardeners who had sweet little plastic bunnies standing, sitting or squatting in their grass and bushes, doing various kinds of things. I remember one beautiful garden I visited which had a reproduction of the famed Winged Victory, done in gold plastic and standing in a bed of plastic daisies. The effect was quite overwhelming.

While your neighbors huff and puff and sweat trying to move heavy rocks into position, you can sit back and smile. You have had the foresight to order artificial rocks for your garden. These rocks come in various sizes and shapes with a choice of fieldstone gray or riverbed brown. And no nicked and bruised knuckles when you surround your flower beds with natural looking plastic stonewall borders.

One of the best new items for the home garden is solar lights. These are available in a variety of styles and since no electricity is needed, they can be placed anywhere. Now you can sit out at night and savor the delight of true garden loveliness.

The Garden Pool

While garden pools were once considered exotic, they are now a common and favorite feature of the home garden. Garden pools, however, can be a chore to keep in good condition unless you follow basic principles of plastic gardening.

The first thing you have to do is select the site for your pool and determine what size you want it to be and how deep. A good choice is 3 feet by 4 feet and a depth of 4 to 6 inches. It is a hard job digging a hole, finding a waterproof liner or pouring cement and takes time. It might be best to have a professional install the pool. You can then concentrate on adding the most important features. You can have fish, water birds and plants, all plastic of course.

Goldfish and koi are the fish usually chosen by pool owners. They do look very elegant swimming around your pool in circles but they have to be fed and they tend to eventually make the water murky. Fortunately there are now "Forever Fish" that while they may "swim" in smaller circles are lifelike plastic. And just this year, one company is offering painted trout made of metal and on sturdy stakes. They do not swim but they do add a decorative touch. If you have room, add a great blue heron to the pool and enjoy the looks of surprise on your visitors when they spot these majestic birds in your yard. By the way, if you don't have a pool, you can put the heron and trout in your flower beds. They will add a special uniqueness and get many admiring glances from passers-by.

Your pool will be complete when you add plastic water lilies, cattails, lily pads and other water plants. A frog or two will add to the scene. You can get frogs in various sizes and positions. They will have to be lightweight to sit on your lily pads. They can always be placed around the edges in playful positions. Plastic turtles can also be used to add to the ambiance.

What if you live in an area where pools are not encouraged because of the drought? This does not need to keep you from enjoying the amenities of a garden pool. You can have a dry pool with fish, birds, frogs, water plants and anything else that you want. You can, if you wish, put a sign up that says "WATER-SAVER POOL" or a similar sentiment. No doubt, you will win applause for your effort in water conservation.

Vegetable and Fruit Plastic Gardening

Too many people who are interested in and practice plastic gardening content themselves with flowers and shrubs when there is another facet of plastic gardening to be done. I myself for many years puttered among my plastic posies until one day a caller said, "Well, I'm surprised that you don't have plastic vegetables!" Her remark was a revelation. It started me thinking, and I decided that I should enlarge my gardening hobby to include such useful things as plastic muskmelons, cucumbers, tomatoes, squash, carrots, peppers, and our old faithful, the onion.

Plastic vegetable gardening technique is slightly different from that of plastic flower gardening. You will need a prepared piece of ground and several yards of your best green, leafy plastic vines.

The vines should be strung along the ground and your plastic melons, cucumbers, squash and peppers fastened at various places to the vine. You may use tape, wire or staples. It looks better and is easier if you fasten the stem end of your vegetable to the vine.

Some vegetables just grow in the ground, so make a little depression and place your carrots, beets, onions or lettuce so they are partially visible.

I know you will also want to get some strings of plastic onions, peppers, tomatoes, and garlic, etc. and hang them around the outside of your house. These not only add touches of color, but proclaim to the world your interest in gardening.

Plastic vegetable gardening has many advantages. For one thing, there is no tiresome weeding or hoeing. You can be in watching television while your neighbor spends hours pulling weeds, getting sunburned, bitten by bugs, and becoming tired and very irritated.

Birds and rabbits won't bother your plastic vegetables, nor will you be bothered by bugs and worms destroying your prize products. While your unhappy neighbor swears at his

 garden predators, you can just smile and go happily on your way secure in your knowledge that your vegetables are safe and unblemished. However, if you really feel you must keep up with the Joneses, toss a handful of plastic worms and bugs into your garden. You won't have any real problems, of course, but it will give you a taste of the anxiety natural gardeners face every day.

There is one feature about plastic vegetable gardening that I particularly like and appreciate. Plastic vegetables begin and end in the garden. Except for planting and storing them at harvest time, they are no trouble. There is no necessity to pick, wash, cook and eat them. If you will notice, natural gardeners spend hours not only in their gardens but in the preparation of the things they have been so foolhardy as to grow.

In addition, you as a plastic vegetable gardener know just how many of each vegetable you have planted, but the natural gardener is always upset by his gardening arithmetic. He either has a surplus which he spends hours running around trying to dispose of to friends and strangers, or he has a shortage and doesn't have enough for any practical use.

You will notice, once you have planted

your plastic vegetable garden, that you have become the envy of the neighborhood. You will not be able to keep from feeling proud as your neighbor stares wistfully over the fence at your large plastic cabbage. You know what he is thinking—and wishing!

Your plastic fruit garden, like your plastic vegetable garden, is a natural outgrowth of your plastic flower days. While there is no limit to the varieties of fruit which you can plant and enjoy, I again caution you to avoid those fruits which are not native to your region. Growing pineapples in the desert is not recommended! I could give you other examples, but I know that you understand the importance of being in step with the natural world around you. Save your exotic fruits for your plastic greenhouse.

Plastic fruits require trees, bushes or small plants. As with vegetables, you will need to fasten your fruit with tape, wire or staples to trees or shrubs. Strawberries do best on small plants close to the ground. It will save time if you purchase plastic strawberry plants rather than just plastic strawberries.

As with plastic vegetables, you will have time for yourself since you do not have to cook or can these fruits. While your neighbor with her natural garden has to spend hours making jellies, jams, pies and preserves, you can be trotting off to the movies or the races, that is, if there is a race track in your town.

Wintertime Gardening

While your natural flower gardener has to content herself with memories of the summer and a few straggly houseplants during the winter months, the plastic flower gardener can enjoy a whole new season of gardening even in the coldest weather.

There are two aspects to winter plastic gardening. Outside where it is cold and miserable, the plastic flower gardener can have lots of greenery arranged in planters. He can look out on this refreshing sight while his neighbor looks out only at barren ground and empty pots.

All kinds of plastic greenery are available in catalogs and stores that sell artificial flowers. A lovely spot of color in your winter garden can come from holly shrubs with their glossy green leaves and bright red berries. If you can't get a shrub, use holly plants. Holiday season is when fir trees are "in" and can be purchased in various sizes from eight inches to five feet. The small ones can be planted in pots or urns and the larger ones planted in the ground. I saw a window box that contained several small fir trees and for a touch of color, the owners had added a plastic bluebird.

Topiary plants bring interest and height to your garden. Putting one on each side of your front door will ensure an air of elegance to your entryway. Guests will smile in approval as they ring your doorbell.

The good thing about these winter greens is that there are no worries about needles or leaves dropping off or turning brown.

Inside, the plastic gardener can have all kinds of house plants. They require no care except for an occasional flick of the dust cloth. In addition, they can be left alone since they don't have to be watered while you go off to Florida, the Bahamas, or Puerto Rico for some warmth and sunshine. Your neighbor will envy you, but she won't be able to join you because she has to stay at home and care for her plants. Incidentally, you can always tell a plastic flower gardener because she has such a jaunty, carefree air.

You don't have to confine yourself to ferns or other green leaf plants indoors, just add flowering plants for color and variety. Geraniums are the most popular plastic flowers available but I have seen other faux flower plants advertised including hydrangeas and ranunculus. African violet plants are also very popular and these require none of the special lighting or care of real plants. Many of these plants come already planted in pots. All you have to do is plump up the leaves a little.

Wintertime is also the time when you can enjoy your rare plants. Put on display your plastic orchids and other exotic plants. It is a time when you can spend many happy hours arranging bouquets of plastic flowers. A bouquet of roses brightens up a winter room. If possible, use opaque vases. If you use a glass, a crumpled sheet of plastic wrap at the bottom will suggest water.

It's always fun to see how you can improve on nature. A good challenge for the winter months is to develop your own hybrid flowers and plants. I have a friend who makes bonsai tree arrangements. You can do the same!

The 21st Century Plastic Gardener

As I indicated at the start of this book, I have used the word "plastic" to refer not just to a type of product but to the concept of faux gardening. Today, flowers, plants and even grass come in a wide choice of material. Thanks to modern design and technology, they have become even more realistic. Birds now have chips that permit them to chirp their songs. Fish, rabbits, frogs and other creatures can fool the eye.

If you want to step beyond the regular boundaries, paint plastic spoons. Paint the handle green and on the back of the bowl paint a color or design. Use waterproof paint. Planted in the ground, a pot or window box, they will last for many years.

Hang old CDs (music ones, not financial ones) from your trees. They will swing, twirl in the wind and reflect the sunlight. You can paint designs on them or leave them *au naturel*. They should be fastened to the tree with sturdy string or wire. They can also be used to decorate fences.

Keep on the lookout for new items for your plastic garden. Get on the mailing lists of garden supply stores and visit your local gardening center. Be the first in your neighborhood to display advanced plastic gardening ideas. Enjoy the looks of disbelief and exclamations of astonishment when people see your accomplishments.

I do recommend Gardener's Supply Company for some of the best and most original garden accessories. While they have mostly things for the natural gardener, they have many objects that will delight the plastic gardener. Their telephone number is 1-800-427-3363 so call for a catalog.

How To Store

Plastic Gardening is more than planting, pruning and painting: it is also storage.

How to store is an essential part of good plastic gardening. It is just as important as the other more glamorous aspects of gardening.

Unlike the natural gardener who must throw away his flowers when they are finished, burn his old leaves or put his bulbs in a dark, cold place, you have the pleasure of saving your flowers and plants for another season. Preparing for storage is work but it is pleasant work. You can listen to appropriate music while doing your tasks (I recommend Percy Grainger's "In A Country Garden").

Flowers

When you bring your individual flowers in either for rotation or at the end of the growing season, there are some things which have to be done. Here is a convenient checklist for you to follow.

1. Remove artificial insects if you have used them. Dust or wash and place in a box appropriately labeled "Bugs."

2. Shake your flowers thoroughly over newspapers. This will remove any natural bugs which may have crept into the folds of your flowers. I know of a few cases of nasty bites suffered by impatient plastic flower gardeners who have skipped this vital step. Shaking the flowers will also dislodge some dust and pieces of mud.

3. If dusting is not enough to restore your flowers to their pristine condition, wash each flower carefully. This can be done by using your kitchen sink spray attachment. If you do not have such a device, just run some warm water in the sink and with a gentle touch and soft cloth wash the flowers. Under no circumstances should you ever put your flowers into the automatic dishwasher or washing machine! The results of such action

can best be described as tragic (the same applies to drying them in your automatic dryer). After washing, flowers should be placed on towels to dry.

4. When flowers are dry, examine each one to see what has to be done in the way of retouching with paint, trimming of ragged edges or taping of torn leaves. It is true that an occasional flower will have to be discarded because of excessive wear due to an unusually heavy rainy or excessively windy season, but this is rare. Your plastic flowers should last you for many seasons.

5. Repairs over, you are ready to store your flowers. You can use cardboard containers, but I recommend clear plastic boxes such as are used to store shoes and blouses. Separate your flowers by species and each species by color. This will save you a great deal of time when the new season of planting comes around. You can go to your boxes and immediately select the flowers that you want without pawing through an entire box of mixed flowers.

6. Keep your boxes on a handy shelf in your garage, your gardening shed, or if you do not have room there, put them on a shelf in one of your closets. This has one advantage—every time you open the closet door, you will be happy to see these bright spots of color staring you in the face. A guest clothes closet is a good place for them, for you can then share this pleasure with your visitors.

Plants

Storing your plants requires a slightly different technique. I am referring to plants which are permanently fastened in pots or bowls. Here is your handy plant storage check list:

1. Repeat Step One as given in your flower check list.

2. If your plants have been used outdoors, examine them carefully for stray bees, spiders and hibernating flies. Remove all of these foreign objects carefully.

3. Wash your leaves and blossoms with a damp cloth. It is not recommended that you put

plants in pots under heavy spray as it tends to loosen the glue with which they are fastened. If you have had your plants indoors, it may be sufficient simply to dust the leaves. Don't forget to dust the piece of plastic which is used to depict plastic dirt in the pot if you are fortunate enough to have an *all* plastic arrangement.

4. Repeat Step Four as given in your flower check list.

5. Put your plants in plastic bags, fasten the plastic securely with tape, and they will be well protected against dust.

6. Place the pots on shelves. You may find, as I do, that it is very convenient to set them in large plastic trays with fairly deep sides. Those sold for use as cat litter boxes are excellent for this purpose.

Garden Accessories

Unless you live in the tropics, your garden accessories will have to be put away for the winter, although there are a few exceptions to this rule.

If your pool has real water, it should be drained. You may want to cover it for protection against the elements. Fish, frogs, water plants and other decorative items should be removed. They should be cleaned, dried and put in boxes. As with your flowers and plants, each object should be checked to see if any repairs or repainting needs to be done.

Other garden accessories should receive similar treatment. Some birds and figures can be left outside if you so wish. First, be sure that they are made of durable material that will withstand the rigors of winter weather. For the most part, it is wiser to put things away. They will last longer and you will be surprised when you see them again in the spring.

You will never regret the time you spend in preparing your garden objects for storage. Careful storage habits means less work at planting time!

The Complete Plastic Gardener And Her (Or His) Garden

In a small treatise such as this, it is not possible to touch on all the facets, the problems, or the delights of plastic gardening. However, I have tried to convey to you the enthusiasm I feel for this wonderful hobby.

Plastic flowers and plants have so many uses. You really feel that you are performing a worthwhile job when you plant, take care of, and use them. For instance, plastic flowers or plants make the ideal gift for the sick person. There is no care, no worry for the invalid when he is presented with a plastic plant. He can enjoy it without worrying how he is going to bribe the aide or the nurse to water it. There is also the advantage that the plastic plant will not deprive the invalid of any precious oxygen. This is especially important when visiting patients who have respiratory complaints. It will not wilt, either, in the hot hospital air.

Plastic plants and flowers are never-ending gifts. You can give a plant to X who in turn gives it to Y who gives it to Z and so on. A natural plant would never survive such treatment, but a plastic plant thrives on and on.

Plastic corsages should be used, for they do not wilt in the heat of the dance. Neither do they take up space in your crowded refrigerator! They have another advantage which is rarely considered: They can *not* be pressed between the leaves of books. How many times have you been annoyed by opening the dictionary and having some old, brown, dried leaves and petals fall out on your best suit?

To give a bouquet of plastic flowers on some festive occasion means that the recipient can have them years after the time has passed and the momentous celebration has faded into the annals of memory. It is always touching to see an old bouquet of plastic flowers in someone's house and hear him say, "This was from my dear mother on the night I graduated from electronics school."

The Complete Plastic Gardener goes all the way. She (or he as the case may be) has plastic shrubs and plastic grass. Not for her the embarrassment of crab grass, bare spots and "molty" shrubbery. She does not have to spend her time fiddling with a soil test kit only to find that the soil is a total loss, but she can plant and enjoy the best of the modern technical world. As it has been said—"Always green, always good."

The complete plastic gardener takes care to have the best in garden accessories and accoutrements. You can always tell a serious plastic gardener by these indications: She will have plastic birds neatly perched in her trees and shrubs, and these will be native birds, not exotic ones. Mushrooms, butterflies and plastic worms will abound in her garden. Her roses will have plastic aphids.

In the house, the complete plastic gardener will have green plants, flowering plants, and an herb garden on her kitchen window sill. Incidentally, that kitchen herb garden will do wonders for your reputation as a gourmet cook. Plastic herb gardens are especially recommended for those cooks who want the reputation, but don't really want to serve their food with a lot of funny-looking leaves and sticks in it.

The complete plastic gardener wants to share her gardening enthusiasm with others. I know I like to share mine, and I am sure that my readers will want to do the same. Let me suggest that you form your own plastic garden club. There is fun and enjoyment in meeting with others who share your hobby of plastic gardening. Remember too, if you start the club, you can insist on being the president as well as the judge of the annual plastic flower show. The possibilities for horticultural prestige are unlimited.

Give plastic gardening the chance it deserves. You will be as surprised as I was at the way your family and friends will accept plastic gardening as the "now" way of growing flowers and plants. If you work at it, you will receive many interesting comments from others as they view your efforts. Why just the other day a visitor saw my garden and exclaimed, "I just can't believe it!"

My wish for you, dear readers, is that you can have the same happy experiences in your plastic gardening career as I have had.

Notes

Notes

Notes

www.ingramcontent.com/pod-product-compliance
Lightning Source LLC
Chambersburg PA
CBHW021026090426
42738CB00007B/923